AN ESSAY ON

MALTA

Casa Ippolita
A ruined cistern, garden and mansion of the early 17th century

AN ESSAY ON MALTA

NIGEL DENNIS

with drawings by
OSBERT LANCASTER

THE VANGUARD PRESS, INC.
424 Madison Avenue New York, N.Y. 10017

Other books by Nigel Dennis

CARDS OF IDENTITY
A HOUSE IN ORDER
EXOTICS (POETRY)
BOYS AND GIRLS COME OUT TO PLAY [A SEA CHANGE]

 ISBN #: 0-8149-0732-6.
Manufactured in the United States of America.

THIS BOOK IS DEDICATED
BY AUTHOR AND ARTIST
TO
DIN L'ART HELWA

The National Trust whose efforts to preserve the landscape and historical buildings of Malta and Gozo have won the admiration of all who love the islands.

My acknowledgments are due to *The Cornhill Magazine* in which a part of Section 2 was originally published.

Contents

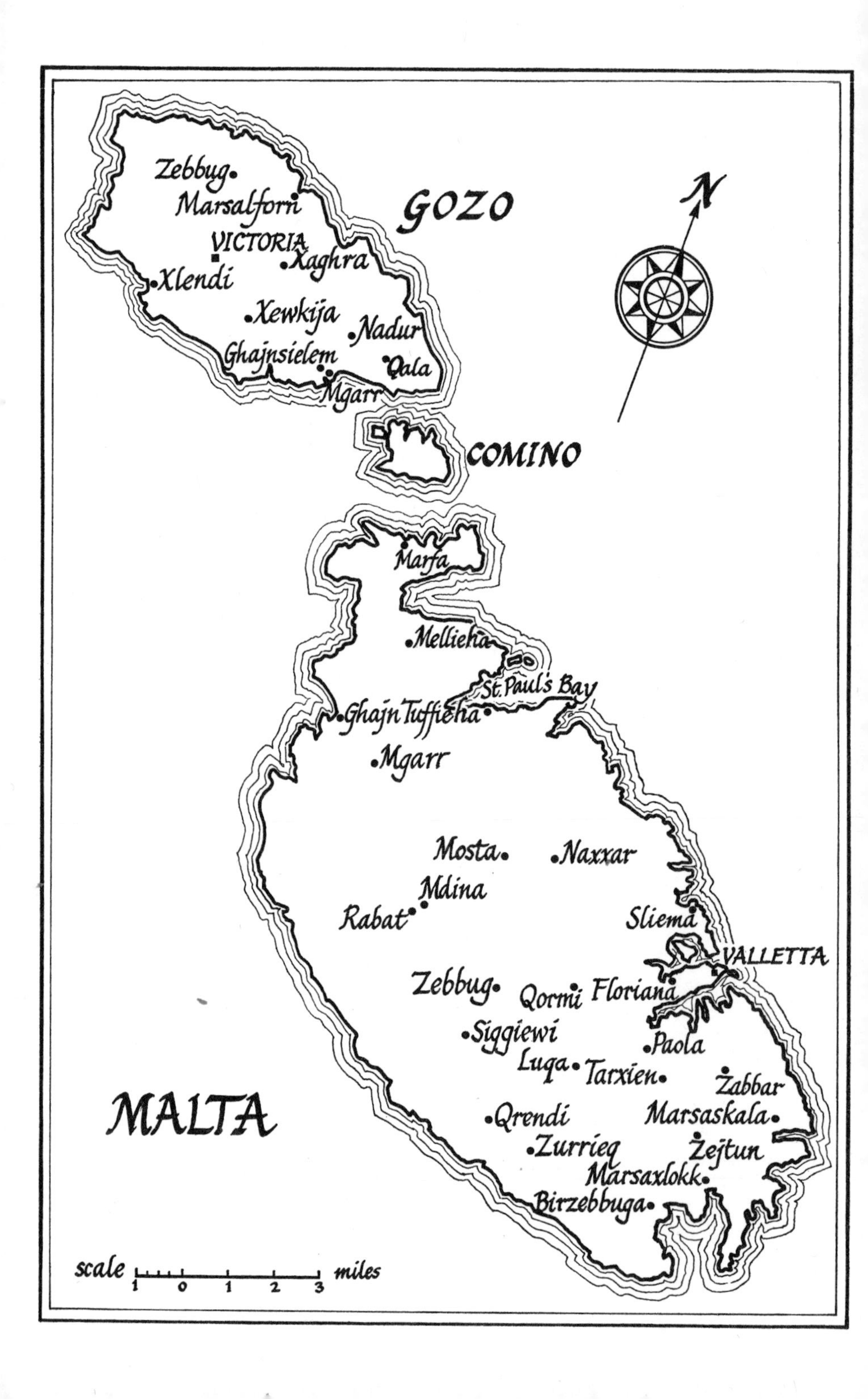
GOZO
N
Zebbug
Marsalforn
VICTORIA
Xaghra
Xlendi
Xewkija
Nadur
Ghajnsielem
Qala
Mgarr
COMINO
Marfa
Mellieha
St. Paul's Bay
Ghajn Tuffieha
Mgarr
Mosta
Naxxar
Mdina
Rabat
Sliema
VALLETTA
Zebbug
Qormi
Floriana
Siggiewi
Paola
Luqa
Tarxien
Żabbar
MALTA
Qrendi
Marsaskala
Zurrieq
Żejtun
Marsaxlokk
Birzebbuga
scale
1 0 1 2 3
miles

Illustrations

OVERTURE BY GIANTS

'Historie', mumbles Manzoni's old pedant, 'may be verilie defined as a mightie war against Time, for, snatching from his hands the years emprisoned, nay already slain by him, she calleth them back unto life, passeth them in review, and rangeth them once more in battle array.' A mighty war indeed—and how much more ingeniously fought today when history may call on so many passionate allies! What hope has Time against a battle array of imaginative heads all disguised with scientific helmets—*demi-monde* warriors such as economists, statisticians, archaeologists, anthropologists, sociologists, psychologists—artists to a man, just like historians, but dedicated sternly to the lab and field? Does Time find the battle easier, by any chance? After all, the allies never agree and are never of the same mind for more than ten or twenty years: not long ago, for instance, they changed all the dates of Maltese pre-history by a thousand years—a long Time by any standard short of eternity.

Among the monuments that suddenly became that much more venerable was the edifice in Malta named Haġar Qim, or 'The Standing Stones'. This remarkable ruin stands on a fine bluff in the south-east of the island looking out over the blue sea; any property developer would tell you that the site was perfectly chosen and that it was a shame to build only one ruin on a spot that could accommodate two hundred villas. But what was this ruin for? The amateur, inspecting its outer wall of huge stones and the connecting rooms laid out in a clover-leaf style, would take for granted that it was for people to live in—a little collection of semi-detached residences, clumped together for safety behind a mighty wall, and with a fine view of any invader coming from sea or land. But we are not allowed to believe this. Haġar Qim, we are assured, was a temple—like almost everything that gets dug up in Malta. Indeed, if there is one thing that we are not allowed to doubt today it is that our ancestors devoted nearly all their time to prayer. They could hardly cut a groove in a wall, let alone paint a naked lady on it, without expressing their devotion to some form of religious experience.

The guide at Haġar Qim will show you the 'tether holes'— holes in the stones connected by a groove through which a rope was passed. He will tell you that these were for tying up 'sacrificial' animals, and he will show you one or two more like them inside, in front of what looks like a useful family table but must be seen as an 'altar'. Any rotund, recessed room must be understood as an 'oracular chamber', and there is no passage that cannot rise to the dignity of an 'aisle'.

How strange it all seems! Of course, it may be true, but one wishes that there could be proof of it. Is it because scientists have no religion themselves that they are so determined to find one among the dead? And if every building was a temple, where did people *live*? You cannot spend your whole life in church.

This question has occurred to the archaeologists too, and it has annoyed them, though it has not, of course, caused them to change their minds. Consultation with their cousins, the statisticians, has shown that for every temple there must be x members of a population. A temple as big as Haġar Qim requires many hundreds of inhabitants: one is not told why, but apparently temple-upkeep demands a large labour-force. The difficulty here is that no such labour-force existed, the archaeologists having decided, in another room, that the population of Malta was extremely small. What to do about this problem except raise it and leave it in the air? To decide that so revered a temple was in fact a block of flats might mean that all archaeology would have to start again. Even to compromise, and suggest that the set-up was a dual-purpose one, like a cathedral close, would be too offensive to be tolerable. Better a non-existent labour-force than a people who did things by halves.

How much easier it was for the historian in the old days when there was no science of archaeology to excite the workings of the romantic imagination! Then, records, hearsay, and eye-witness evidence were the only things that counted, and these were usually present in abundance. The old historian had a stern eye and a severe, objective mind; unlike today's demi-scientist he had no respect for primitive magic. He did not dismiss all ritual rain-making as nonsense, but he had none of the pious devotion to it that marks the pre-historian of today. In many ways, he did not take pre-historic people so seriously either, chiefly because it never occurred to him that that is what they were. When a man is using the Old Testament and the works of Homer as his documentary sources, he sees the people involved as people who are demonstrably inside history rather than preparing the way for it: their behaviour, odd as it often is, is clearly narrated in the apposite documents, and there is no need at all for the old historian to give way to the fanciful dreaming that marks the pre-historian of today. Finally, feeling no desire to re-discover himself among the people of yore, he need not struggle to put himself 'in their place'—always the unkindest of all struggles in that the place in which the dead are is the very one from which they can never answer back.

The hero of our story, Commendatore Giacomo Abela, generally known as 'The Father of Maltese History', was just such an old, severe historian. A distinguished Brother of the Sacred Order of St. John of Jerusalem, he was the first native historian of his country. Trained in the law at the University of Bologna, his main criterion as an historian was what he called 'indubitable evidence'. His famous *Discrittione di Malta, Isola nel Mare Siciliano* was written in Italian in his old age and published in Valletta in 1647: this makes him contemporary with Aubrey and Clarendon. His account of Malta's early history was based on the best 'indubitable evidence' of his day, and if it strikes the reader as inaccurate in some respects, he should not suppose it to be any more credulous and fanciful than the ever-changing fairy-tales that we are asked to believe today.

Malta's first inhabitants, Abela tells us, were Noah's grandsons, who settled in the islands after the Flood. We may assume them to have been the children of Shem, that son of Noah who was the first King of Sipontum in Calabria. These Biblical grandsons were joined in Malta by two sorts of Giants, the common-or-garden species of Calabria, and the notorious one-eyed Cyclopes of Sicily. The latter were the ancestors of that Giant tribe known as the Phoeacians, who traced their descent from King Eurimedonte, King of the Giants, whose immense daughter, Peribea, married Nausitoo, son of Poseidon. It was the Phoeacians who gave Malta its first name, Iperia, and they remained in the islands for a long time in company with other Giants descended from Japheth, the Prophet Elisha, and Polyphemus. But at last, warfare broke out among the Giants in the area and caused the Phoeacians to be expelled to Corfu by the Cyclopes. However, Abela, who is always cautious in coming to conclusions, brings to our attention the alternative put forward emphatically by the historian Cluverio—that 'the Phoeaci of Iperia . . . were defeated not by Cyclopes, or Giants, but by the Phoenicians'. If so, the conquerors were of normal size, of Egyptian descent (in Abela's view), and left their home at Thebes to found the city of Tyre 'in about the last years of Moses' life'. Certainly, they had reached Malta, which they re-named Ogygia, long before Ulysses had landed at Gozo ('the island of Calypso') and settled for seven years in the Grotto which is one of the tourist attractions of the present day.

Once the Phoenicians appear on the horizon in the history of a Mediterranean country, a certain sobriety seems to appear with them. Instead of one-eyed Giants, prophets, Nymphs, and antediluvians, we have straightforward businessmen engaged in nothing more exotic than buying and selling. But, as in Sicily and Calabria, we must expect in Malta a certain cross-current of mysterious visitors amidst the Phoenician business offices. Other Greeks are bound to follow Ulysses to the islands, if only to establish a 'Classical' tie with antiquity; the odd Trojan is sure to turn up in passing to Rome with Aeneas; and St. Paul, also on his way to Rome, may be accompanied by Mark, Luke and John. Sometimes, too, the *Odyssey* gets transposed into early Christian hagiology, and we find St. Agatha of Catania—always a revered saint in Sicily, Calabria, and Malta—doing duty for Penelope and escaping her Sicilian suitor by unravelling at night in a Maltese cave the veil she spins by day. But these are minor complications: once the

Phoenicians have fallen into place, the Carthaginians follow quite naturally; after which it is a mere step to the Romans, the Punic Wars, and other commonplaces of ancient history.

But is Abela prepared to accept all this, simply because it has all been recorded? Certainly not! He has gone out into the 'field' himself, like his modern brother; he has inspected the great ruin of Haġar Qim and that other megalithic edifice, in Gozo, known as Ġgantija. 'With our own eyes', he tells us, he has looked on these, and like the Anglo-Saxon poet who looked with awe on the bramble and ivy tangled remains of Roman Bath, he has asked himself: who but Giants could have been here, for who but Giants could have built so gigantically? Here is confirmation of the literary evidence; here before one's very eyes is 'indubitable evidence of the fact that the first inhabitants of Malta were of the race of Giants'. Not so far away, one can even see what appear to be the Giants' graves: one of these is so large that it is now being used as 'a small orchard'. Finally, there are two teeth that could only have come from gigantic jaws: one of these colossal molars is owned by Abela himself, the other by his antiquarian friend, Count —. A life-size engraving of one of these teeth is presented in the *Discrittione*; it measures no less than two inches from root to tip.

Contemporary Maltese historians express great reverence for the 'Father' of their history, but with a carping, even apologetic air. They doubt that he maintained the highest possible modern standards in reaching the wrongest possible conclusions; nor are they comforted by the fact that, like all of us, he went straight to the source and found inevitably the absolute assurance he was looking for. Certainly, it is hard to assess an historian who pins on Giants the molars of an herbivorous mammal and reckons the size of a people in terms of their building blocks: if the building of immense places of worship were the criterion, the Maltese would be Giants even today. The fact is that the 'Father' is often untrustworthy when he by-passes the mere written word and sticks absolutely to facts.

The absolute accuracy of his observations and the modest gravity with which he presents the misconceptions that his accuracy creates, are among Abela's most human and up-to-date qualities. The histories of all countries must always be impositions of the present upon the past, with the facts of yesterday shaped by the fancies of today; but Malta is most particularly a country where history has had to be re-invented continuously. Within its tiny area there is so much to be discovered that the effort to do so is quite discouraged: with so much known to be there, no urgency is felt about bringing it to the surface. Nonetheless, each generation makes its spasmodic attacks on the subterranean mysteries, and each emerges with its own story; but with each discovery the mysteries take on another aspect and require the story to be re-told. No story of Malta—of its pre-history, its people, even its language—holds water for very long; each in its turn must become as fanciful in its notions as Abela was in his. A litter of discarded theories trails over the whole island like a mad paper-chase, a grief to the devout, an amusement to the sceptic.

Where Abela differs from many theoreticians is in his readiness to distinguish as clearly as he can between fact and fable. He is fond of folk-lore but he never starts, as many do today, with the conviction that if people have believed something long enough, nothing remains but to find means of proving it correct.† His careful approach is shown in a famous passage of the *Discrittione* that describes the fate of the village of Maqluba, which is Maltese for topsy-turvy, or upside down. This village, which is near the sea, disappeared in ancient times when its stone floor collapsed. Abela, who knew nothing of 'faults' and subsidences, writes as follows:

'*MaKluba.* Topsy turvy, where there is a huge chasm below the Casal of *Krendi*; the circumference of the mouth of this is 152 canes. The depth is such that those at the bottom look like Pygmies; nonetheless, 70 years ago a vineyard with many trees was planted down there. The fertility of the soil, helped in winter

† Folk-lore creates its fantasies more slowly than gossip; nonetheless, it works fast. In 1920, Maurice Magnus killed himself with a dose of cyanide in the upper room of a small house in Mdina. Already, the inhabitants of the street will assure you that the house is 'haunted'—by the ghost of a Knight of St. John who hanged himself there 'hundreds of years ago'. Thus, it has taken only half a century to change a memorable event into an immemorial invention.

by copious quantities of water that flooded everything but always drained away through crevices in the surrounding rocks, and walled off from the cold winds, but still enjoying ample sunshine, combined to produce the tastiest and sweetest fruits. Access to the place is very difficult, particularly on account of the loose rocks, although the proprietor of the vineyard and his gardeners have made foot and hand holes to get holds on and manage to carry baskets of fruit to the top. It is a firm and undoubted tradition among almost all Maltese that there stood here at one time long ago a Casal whose inhabitants did not live according to the will of God, and by their weakness of faith and, indubitably, their misdeeds, roused His ire, and caused Him, by means of an earthquake or some other method, to plunge the whole village into the ground. His Divine Majesty, in his exact justice, left only the ancient church dedicated to St. Matthew standing on the brink, and saved therein only one poor, but pious, woman who had repeatedly called on the villagers and pleaded with them to change their ways if they were to escape the punishment they could expect from Divine justice. As to the date of this event, we can only conjecture that it was before the Saracens conquered the island. And as to what happened exactly, we have no assurance save that which is supplied by the tradition itself. However, there is manifest evidence that buildings stood here, and upon the very ground that was swallowed up at the time, and this is the half of a cistern, still showing its caulking, on the brink, which we have seen and studied many times, and the other half of which is flung down in fragments over the whole chasm. Moreover, the very name of *MaKluba* confirms the said tradition; the aforementioned Church has been held until today by the people in deep devotion; its floor in former days was lashed to the rock with what was certainly bitumen, or crushed chalk stone fragments, all mixed with other materials, and giving it such a lustre as to make it seem made of porphyry; which paving we have not seen for many years: at present there is only the excavation, or bed, over which this mixture was once spread. In the same Church there is a most beautiful festa every year which draws numerous people not only for reasons of piety but out of curiosity and the beauty of the place, which contributes not a little to the advantage and profit of the gardener, who, at this time of celebration on the 21st September, sells huge quantities of his grapes and fruit.'

The great chasm still exists as such today. But there is no longer any garden at the bottom, only a profusion of dead fruit trees, vigorous bamboos and, appropriately, green bay trees of great size. The steps cut by the gardener are broken and cracked, the handholds are eroded and worn. A tiny fragment of the old church still stands at the very brink, but what is really surprising is to see the half of the cistern, standing exactly as Abela described it and still 'showing its caulking'; at one corner one may still see the channel through which the cistern filled from the roof of the house that once stood above it. One does not leave Maqluba amused by the naivety of the recorder of divine legends, but impressed by the precision of the recorder of facts.

Today's pre-historian is less sceptical than Abela and has less desire to take folk-lore with a grain of salt. Legend, he tells us, cannot lie: it can only express, in an archaic tongue, information that must be translated into modern language. This attitude is obviously based more on faith than science and takes no account of the fact that the translator is convinced before he begins to translate: the original only serves to bear out what the translator has invented. However, in Abela's case, this capricious method has been applied with some success. Abela's language, says the archaeologist, was of his day, but what it represents in translation is perfectly up-to-date. The first inhabitants of Malta did, indeed, come originally from the territory of Noah, which was Anatolia. The sherds of their characteristic pottery provide 'indubitable evidence' that they travelled to Malta by way of Calabria and Sicily. Abela's only mistake was to see as Giants what must be grasped as pots.

The weakness of this argument is that the archaeologist stands his pots on the premise that Malta can be seen from Sicily and was therefore a visible attraction to the Neolithic pot-bearer. Many other conclusions about the early Maltese settlements are built on this visual premise. They are all invalid because Malta cannot be seen from Sicily at all.

* * * * *

This account of the settling of Malta is of importance in understanding Maltese history. To put it shortly, Malta and her historians have spent hundreds of years embracing Europe and the Holy Land and rebuffing Africa. In their own eyes, they have been to Southern Europe what Vienna has been to Eastern—the last, lonely fortress of Christianity. They have picked and chosen with care the sources of their origin, and many of the distortions that mark their written history and their popular beliefs come from the determination they have shown to look with disdain on the land of Numidia and Barbary. That their islands lie virtually in the Gulf of Tripoli, only 200 miles from Tunis and farther south than Cape Bon, has not impressed them at all, nor have they ever shown the smallest desire to claim a share in a Christian region that was once greater and more influential than any other—the Africa of St. Augustine, St. Cyprian, and Tertullian. The stream they recognise rises in the Holy Land and reaches them by way of Sicily and Southern Italy; it is joined, acceptably enough, by the ancient, classical odysseys of Homer because these are the source of European civilisation. That the beauty of their countryside and its stone farmhouses is as much African as it is Levantine has never moved them because they have never noticed it: architecture, to the Maltese, has always been essentially urban, Christian, and baroque.

All the opening pages of Abela's *Discrittione* express exactly this preoccupation with the European world. The reader who fails to understand this will wonder why on earth such a sober historian should devote so much space to the apparently simple question: where *is* Malta? But Abela calls upon all possible authorities, ancient and modern, including Ptolemy, Homer, Herodotus, Thucydides, Diodorus Siculos, and Ovid to prove that the Maltese islands are 'closer to Sicily than to Africa'. Geographers, cosmographers, professors of many nations, sea-captains, ship-wrecked mariners are all called upon to confirm Malta's whereabouts, and the very names on the old maps of the Western Mediterranean are accepted or refuted according as to whether they tally with or deny the European connection. One of Abela's trump cards is the school 'cosmography' of one Giovanni Domenico Feltri, which puts to Italian students the question: 'What are the islands surrounding Italy?' and replies:

In the Tuscan Sea, Elba, Procida, Ischia.
In the Sicilian Sea, the islands Liparee, Malta.
In the Adriatic Sea, S. Maria di Triemete, Vinegia,
and the islands about Vinegia.

Can one fail to conclude, Abela asks, that that which lies in the Sicilian Sea must be Sicilian, that what is Sicilian must be Italian, and that what is Italian is 'thus in Europe'? 'Nor can we ascertain', he goes on, 'why that worthy historian of our unconquerable Order, Giacomo Bosio, can declare that Ptolemy, Pliny, Mela, Strabo, and (he says) almost all cosmographers and geographers place the island of Malta in Africa, and under the Province of Numidia'. After showing that they do nothing of the sort and that they regard Malta as an island in 'the high seas', he stresses that Malta 'is 200 miles away, and not 190, as Bosio would have us believe, from the nearest port of the [African] continent', whereas the distance between Malta and the tower of the small Sicilian promontory of Pozzallo is 60 miles, and not, as Strabo has it, 88. Who, then, with such evidence behind him would dare to deny the stirring description of Malta supplied by the poet Francesco della Valle:

The unconquerable last outpost of Italy
That divides the sea of the great Sicanian Throne
Among the heroes of the White and Sacred Cross,
Crying Hosanna amid the fulminations of battle?

It would be absurd to reject entirely Abela's struggle to dissociate Malta from Africa. No struggle is needed to show the long, intimate connection that has bound Malta to Europe for a larger part of its history. But the link with Africa is much too strong to be denied or played down in discussing an island whose native language is essentially Semitic and whose place-names, with a mere handful of Romance exceptions, present the philologist with nothing but fascinating Semitic puzzles. How does one explain this indubitable fact; how can one answer the question why the place-names and language of Sicily are as much Sicilian as those of Malta are Semitic, and this despite the fact that both islands were subject to the Arabs over the same period of time (A.D. 870 to 1090)?

Abela was well aware of this question, as all Maltese historians have been ever since. He answers it by saying that when the Arabs invaded Malta, which was then, he believes, a Christian country under Byzantine rule, the Maltese nobles took to their ships and fled to Constantinople. Only the peasants remained, and they, he says, 'were obliged to accept the conquerors' language, and this the more probably because they were not, in all likelihood, trained to the pen, which is the guardian of native idiom'. Such, he says, was not the situation in those parts of Sicily and Italy that were conquered by the Arabs: there, more literate people remained behind, so that the established language continued to be written and generally spoken.

This is certainly a topsy-turvy argument which arises, ultimately, out of Abela's rejection of pagan Africa. It is also quite at variance with what generally happens when a country is conquered. The native idiom is never guarded by the educated; it is maintained through thick and thin by the ignorant. It is the nobles who make haste to learn their overlord's language; it is the vulgar who are slowest to change their tongue and have the least need to do so. For many centuries the upper class families of Malta have made themselves at home first in the Italian language of Church and Law and then in English; by doing so, they have taken their place in the government of both Church and State. Often, they have not spoken Maltese at all, except a little to their servants. They have always been obliged to do this, because their servants have understood no language but the ancient 'native idiom'.

Can we believe, then, that the Arabs conquered a country of

peasants who spoke a sort of dog-Latin (as Abela suggests) and converted their speech into a basically Semitic one during the two hundred years of Arab occupation? It is highly improbable, and those who follow Abela in the struggle to orientate Malta in Byzantine and Latin exclusiveness have tried to make his argument sound better by suggesting that the Arab influence in Malta continued for at least a further two hundred years after the Norman conquest of 1087, much as Phoenician influence is said to have continued after the Roman conquest. Thus the common people had four hundred years in which to change their speech, which would be time enough even for the most illiterate.

Behind all such arguments lies the desire to posit a Christian Malta from as early a date as possible. Yet there are more plausible alternatives to consider. One is that the Maltese were a people of Levantine or North African stock when the Arabs arrived and that they spoke a language somewhat similar to that of their conquerors. This language, says one authority,† was probably Punic, 'a Semitic off-shoot of Phoenician', and had been the language of Malta not only in Phoenician times but throughout the long periods of Carthaginian and Roman rule: it gave way 'much more easily than Latin or Greek before the onrush of Arabic words and names'. As to the toponymy, all that the Arabs had to do was 'adapt local place-names to their Arabic phonetics, just as English residents still do'. It is also possible that the Maltese, whatever language they spoke, were few in number when the Arabs came, and that the island was thoroughly colonized by the invaders. What it was in respect to religion when the Normans came, nobody has ever found out: even the fact that 200 years later, in 1240, the official records of Messina gave the number of 'Saracen' families in Malta as 836, the Christian as 250, the Jewish as 39, has not been of much use to historians because there are different ways of understanding these figures.

The same authority warns all investigators against riding particular hobby-horses in the matter of the Maltese race and language. Anyone who reads the numerous books and pamphlets on these

† J. Aquilina: *Papers in Maltese Linguistics*, Royal University of Malta (1961).

The Citadel, Gozo.

matters will think this a wise warning, so various are the theories and arguments. The movements of the so-called 'Mediterranean Race' and their successors in Neolithic times and later are so uncertain and yet so complicated that the explaining of them leads only from one obsession to another. Some choose to think that there is no place like Malta; it is entirely unique. Others argue that it is much like everywhere else—originally one link in a chain of people moving westwards continuously from the eastern Mediterranean, the Levant, or the headwaters of the Nile. Language, pottery, skull measurements, the incidence of blue eyes (in Malta), of grey (in Gozo) can all be called on to prove, say, a close relationship with the fishermen of Galway, or a curious expression still to be heard in Worcestershire. From time to time, speculation is caught short by a totally-unexpected discovery—such as that of the only skull dug up under Haġar Qim, which proved to be a Negro's. As this gentleman's head fitted no place in the theories of anybody else's, room was bound to be invented for it; this was done by an Englishman who suggested that the Maltese, as devout then as now, had worshipped their dark, mysterious visitor. Soon, their devotion grew so intense that they had exclaimed: 'Oh, I could eat you up!' and, by suiting the action to the word, showed how easy it was even in Neolithic times to allow religious enthusiasm to go too far.

One learns two important lessons from all this curious reading. One is that though final answers are difficult to find anywhere, in Malta they are never found at all: anything interesting is always inexplicable. The second lesson is that references to peoples and places usually means nothing at all. There is, for example, a legend in Tunisia which says that that country was the homeland of the Maltese. But what was Tunisia in those days, and what people lived there? Another legend says that the Maltese came from Mount Carmel; this only provokes the same question. What is odd is that both legends may be approximately true. If for Mount Carmel we read Phoenicians and proto-Phoenicians, and for Tunisia Carthaginians, we may not be far off. The impossibility of really solving such problems is due to the fact that the movements of peoples in the Levant and North Africa were so various and continuous that virtually no such thing as an 'origin' can be posited dogmatically.

One who thought otherwise was Louis de Boisgelin, a Knight of the Order of St. John. Writing of the Maltese in 1803, he said:

> 'The Maltese, though continually subject to different nations have always preserved their original character; which sufficiently proves their descent, and, at the same time, shews that they have mixed very little with any of the people who have by turns governed their country.
>
> 'Their countenances announce an African origin. They are short, strong, plump, with curled hair, flat noses, turned up lips, and the colour of their skins is the same as that of the inhabitants of the states of Barbary: their language is also so nearly the same, that they perfectly understand each other.'

Here is a statement from the African school as emphatic as any ever made by the European school—and with no evidence of any sort to support it: even the reference to the language is extravagant. The 'curled hair' of the Maltese is no more African than that of Sicily and Italy, and more often than not it is not curled at all but is a magnificent shock of long, straight hair, made fascinating in the women by the fact that its rich blackness is strongly tinged with a russet tone: only rarely has it the raven black of more northern people. The lips are not unduly 'turned up', and as for Boisgelin's 'flat noses', they are an attempt to rob Malta of one of its greatest glories. For the student of noses, Malta is a perfect paradise: one may find in the poorest alleys of the island the finest noses the world can show. Superbly straight or aquiline, but always finely and perfectly modelled, these noses may be called 'Greek' or 'Roman' for convenience; but in fact they seem to share all the elegance and dignity of the noses found on Assyrian and Hittite reliefs. When such noses are combined, as they often are, with the abundant russet-tinted black hair, very large dark eyes and a tiny, slim figure, the result is immensely striking and extremely beautiful. True, such a small graceful gazelle easily becomes a stout little deer as she grows older, but fashion, diet, and the reduction in the number of her children from a dozen-odd to a handful, is sure to correct in the poorer people a tendency that has long been in process of correction among the richer. There is no better corrective to the shape of the figure than an excess of immodesty: what is enjoined by the pastoral letter is quickly expunged by the swimsuit.

The pre-historical remains of Malta have only two things to tell us about how the Maltese figure fared in the olden days and what the people looked like. Two sorts of statues, statuettes and figurines are found, and although both sorts may be found together, each entirely contradicts the other. One sort would seem to be entirely representational: pressed out in clay, often very crudely, or cut out of stone, it represents a figure of ordinary proportions with nothing very interesting about it. Such figures are usually classed as votives, some of them showing signs of serious illness and swollen or wasted parts. They are only a few inches high.

The other sort is not only interesting but includes the greatest triumphs of Maltese sculpture. They are exercises in obesity, and the degree to which they represent exaggeratedly a living figure cannot be ascertained at all. Classed recklessly as 'priestesses' and 'goddesses', they do not, in fact, even deign to state whether they are men or women. The great Maltese scholar, Sir Themistocles Zammit, judging by the relative fatness or rotundity of the chests and the absence or presence of nipples, decided that most of them are men. But the general observer takes for granted that all of them are women, their crossed or tucked-up legs suggesting immediately to the modern eye a serene femininity of posture.

Zammit also pointed out most properly that they must not be classified as steatopygous, in that the protrusion of the behind is neither here nor there in a figure that is shaped entirely in protuberant masses. He saw with a very sharp eye that these figures are, as it were, cut from the living fat, and that their remarkable beauty is due to the marvellous way in which their obese limbs have been related and arranged. A few of the standing figures may once have been as much as nine feet in height; but it is the smaller seated and reclining ones that shed the stiffness of the statuesque and present their voluminous folds with such a charming blend of dignity, suppleness, and self-contentment: this is enhanced by the feet and hands being proportionately tiny. Dismissed by many for years as 'ridiculous', 'grotesque', and even 'disgusting', their beauty is only appreciated if they are seen as figments of an artist's dream, obviously due to a preponderating style but open to anybody's guess as to religious significance or representation of a racial type. None of the seated ones have heads; all that remains between the shoulders are the sockets and pin-holes to which heads were once attached: these, it would seem, were able to turn and to nod like a doll's.

Some of these so-called 'Fat Ladies' have lost their marvellous rotundity by having been carved as it were sideways, instead of in depth; the fatness protrudes at their sides as if they had been squeezed in a press, when warm, and left to cool: the flatness of back that results suggests that these were seated on a ledge and set tight against a wall. Time and centuries of interment have roughened and pitted the surface of all the 'Fat Ladies', so that when one is walking on the cliffs and looking down on the stone forms that have been rounded and pitted by the waves, one can often enjoy the pleasant illusion that the rocks and the rounder ladies are all of a piece and that the Neolithic sculptor took his instructions from the sea. However, as many ladies of the same form may still be found in any Maltese village street, we need not call on the sea for an inspiration that was probably close to hand.

Where is Malta? is a question that can be answered: *Who are the Maltese*? is quite unanswerable. We read in the old histories of pirate raids in which virtually all the inhabitants of Gozo were carried off into slavery: by whom were they replaced? We read of the planting of Italian colonies; we know that large numbers of Sicilian workmen were imported by the Knights. No less than 4,000 Rhodians—surely a greatly exaggerated number—are said to have accompanied the Knights to their new home. And yet, it would be wrong to conclude that the result is a Mediterranean hybrid of no recognisable stock. A distinct population is not made only by the mixed stocks of a people; it is made by inherited habits, language, and traditional beliefs. Language alone—its origins, its vocabulary—can seem to be the most decisive racial factor, as was the case in the furious quarrel that divided the Maltese for generations into pro-Italians and pro-Phoenicians. A new and interesting aspect of this quarrel appeared when Zammit suggested that the determining element was to be found in grammar, rather than words. 'Grammar resists all corruption . . . for though languages may get mixed in their vocabulary they can never be mixed in their grammar.' More recently, Aquilina has boldly extended this principle to the Maltese stock itself, writing: 'The Armenoid type (i.e. the Anatolian, or Hittite) has persisted to this very time in spite of all outside influences very much as the Semitic base of Maltese grammar has persisted in spite of the preponderating number of loan-words from Romance sources.'

NOBLES, PIRATES AND PECULIAR NAMES

Siġġiewi

There were histories of Malta long before Abela's day. They began to appear after the Great Siege of 1565, when all Europe became interested suddenly in the distant island that had thrown back the Infidels in the south. But this brought into Maltese history the clerical bias that runs through Abela and persists even today: by now, it has been established for so many centuries that it is not so much biased as traditional and ordinary. The tendency is to push Maltese Christianity farther and farther back in time—to let Malta share the Christian persecutions of the Romans, to become Byzantine Christians at the division of the Empire, to draw a line that wavers, but never disappears, from the landing of St. Paul in A.D. 43 to the Norman conquest a thousand years later. The Arab conquest is a serious intrusion into this traditional view and is dealt with much as if it were a Roman persecution. As Abela, too, believed, Arab rule was a cruel, alien yoke under which the Christian island suffered bitterly, struggling to maintain a faith that the conquerors were determined to wipe out. The supposed rapture with which Roger the Norman was received is still thought to indicate the misery of Christian Malta under the Arabs; moreover, there is reason to suppose that by a simple telescoping of history, the real suffering of the Maltese many centuries later at the hands of African corsairs and pirates has been transferred backwards in time to include the period of Arab domination. Only Boisgelin flatly denies this traditional view of the Arab occupation:

> 'During the whole of the time they inhabited Malta, they treated the Christian religion and its ministers with proper respect, and were humane and just in their conduct towards the inhabitants, upon whom they laid no taxes . . . The Arabs having . . . instructed them in piracy, their own experience perfected them in the business; and the Maltese became, indeed still are, the ablest corsairs in the Mediterranean.'

In truth, what happened in Malta under the Arabs is known to nobody. Tradition has preferred the heavy yoke of Abela to Boisgelin's contented centuries of merry piracy, and Maltese historians have shown no desire to unravel by day the yarns that religion has spun by night. Though the Arabs come under many different names in the passing of the centuries—Saracens, Turks, Infidels, Barbarians, Moors, Corsairs—they have always had to bear the onus of a religious intolerance that should more often be laid on the Christians of Europe. The very Order of St. John of Jerusalem, of which Abela was Vice Chancellor, owed its beginnings to the tolerance of the Caliphs, who permitted the original hospice to establish itself in Jerusalem in the 11th century, to care for the thousands of Christian pilgrims who travelled to the Church of the Holy Sepulchre. The Maltese were under the Arabs at this time;

their liberation (if such it was) by Roger the Norman coincided by all but two years with the 'liberation' of Jerusalem by the First Crusade in 1099. History records the atrocious massacre of infidels that followed the capture of Jerusalem; it also records that not a single Arab place of worship was left standing by the Normans after their conquest of Sicily. How the Arabs behaved in Malta is a question that may never be answered; but at least the historian is sufficiently well-informed today not to visit on Moslems alone an intolerance and savagery that was a distinguishing mark of Christian knighthood.

As has been noted, the Malta to which the Carthaginians came was, in Abela's eyes, 'undoubtedly' a country of Greeks, and was still such a country under the Romans when St. Paul landed on the island. Place-names and surnames in Malta confirm a strong Greek presence in the island from early times, but leave unanswered the interesting question, what sort of Greeks? That some should have come to Malta from Byzantium is likely enough; that many more should have come already from the Greek colonies in Sicily and Calabria is virtually certain. And yet, there has been not the smallest trace of Greek colonisation in Malta—no evidence whatever of their physical presence. How is this to be explained?

First, we may consider the fact that there is a similar absence of Greek remains in Western Sicily. The reason for this is that the colonists of ancient Greece never entered the western part of Sicily, which was held by the Phoenicians and the Carthaginians until the Roman conquest in the Punic Wars. The history of Malta was probably the same: held by the Phoenicians and Carthaginians as a way-station to their Sicilian ports, it never became a Greek colony.

Consideration might also be given to the thought that some of the Maltese 'Greeks' were, in fact, North Africans. By A.D. 700, we are told:

> 'Arab chroniclers were able to report that "there is no longer found in Ifriqiya either Greeks or Berbers disposed to resist". The "Greeks" included the Byzantines, the Italians, and the

Romanised Africans; the Berbers, all those mountain and desert tribes who occupied North Africa down to the Sahara Desert.'†

If such was the case with the 'Greeks' of Malta, it would strengthen greatly the argument of those who believe that when the Arabs came, they found a people whose language had long been basically the same as their own.

* * * * *

Until recent years, all Maltese history has been clerical history, except when politicians and foreigners have written it. Today, a certain division is apparent between the clerical historian and the lay professor, with the cleric still disposed to trace a Christian and

† James Wellard, *Lost Worlds of Africa* (1967). Wellard also tells us that the Moslem Tuaregs of Libya, who were probably Christians long ago, still refer to God as *Mesi*— 'thought to be a variant of "Messiah"'. The Maltese reverse this process and still call God *Alla* (their Messiah is the Italianate *Messija*). Their interesting word for father is *missir*, supposedly a corruption of Siculo-Norman French (cf. *m'sieur*), though mother enjoys the fruity, Semitic title of *omm* (Arabic; Sumerian: *umm*). With Greek *Messias* and Aramaic *Meshiha* to hand, it seems strange that father should have to wait for the Normans to get his name: it must always have taken at least one *missir* to make an *omm*.

Other origins that have been suggested for this strange word are derivations from the Semitic verbs *sar* (to generate) and *issir* (to ripen, to slide into): Aquilina, however, accepts the Romance origin.

European line from early times to the present day and the professor taking more pride in following whatever line is indicated by language and archaeology. Each draws on Abela according to his needs, but the cleric is still much closer to his 17th century predecessor than the professor is. One reason for this is that though Abela could be described as a religious historian, he could never be described as an historian of the Maltese. His true interest was in the people who were the least Maltese of all—the upper class and the higher clergy. 'There were always nobles in Our City,' he says proudly, but these nobles are precisely the people in whom we are least interested today, the speech of the peasant or the relics of the pre-historic villager exciting our imagination more than the genealogies of the richer pirates. Nonetheless, we get two sorts of useful information from Abela's long section on Malta's nobility, the first being the lively picture it provides not of Malta as a lonely island but of Malta as part of a variegated Mediterranean empire ruled from Spain and Sicily.

Some of the personages he mentions are Maltese by birth and go to the continent to make their fortunes: granted baronies and property by the Spanish and Hohenstaufen Emperors, they establish themselves in Sicily and Calabria and never return to Malta. But more often, the movement is the other way. The Norman Conquest of Malta is like that of England in that the best people must start their pedigrees with it; the difference is that the 'Normans' who came to Malta were 'Normans, Sicilians, Calabrians, and other Italians'. They were followed to Malta by soldiers of fortune drawn from as far afield as Greece, Germany, Flanders, France, Hungary, and many parts of Spain: a 'parchment signed with the very hand of King Alfonso in favour of Bartolomeo Abela' was the historian's earliest prized possession among his family documents. Dated 15th March, 1443, it confirmed the rights and antiquity of the family of d'Abella, or D'Abel, rightful descendants of a Catalonian soldier from the time of the Aragonese 'Conquest' of Malta.

This ancestor was one of the 'two hundred good Catalonian soldiers' supposedly posted in Malta under General Roger di

Auberge de Castille and Church of St. Catherine of Italy, Valletta

Lorio by King Peter of Aragon and chief among the legendary founders of the Maltese nobility: '. . . for they founded a diversity of houses, such as Sorribes, Caldes, Cardona, Mompalau, Xirica, Barbarà, Rioles, Sans, Pelligrino, Ferriol, Portella, Begliera, Frontina, Mediona, and others.' Treated as 'true Sicilian subjects', they found wives 'among the families of Maltese merchants', and they settled on lands, all carefully listed by Abela, granted them by their Swabian, French and Aragonese overlords. In this way, they replaced the Maltese 'nobles' who had escaped to Byzantium when the Arabs came.

'Finally, the motive which brought various nobles to Malta to establish their houses there was the sea traffic, with the great opportunity it provided to take arms against the infidel with galleys and galley slaves and other weapons of the times.' To this noble motive was joined the practical one of bringing home to Malta plunder and booty which, saving only that which was apportioned to the crown, 'made many of them rich, with an abundance of slaves and other goods'. And it was thus, Abela concludes, that Malta was 'rehabilitated' after the Arab occupation, and not, as has been shamefully suggested and quite without foundation, 'by bandits, or by exiles sent there as punishment for their misdeeds'.

* * * * *

Where are the noble names today? A few have survived in noble lines; most have long outlived the families that brought them and have spread down into the whole community. There, they have joined with a diversity of names that manage to be at once typically Maltese and yet demonstrably European, Levantine, and African. Abela's list of noble names of 1647 is superseded now by the Telephone Directory: there, we find a collection of fascinating names that call the roll of Maltese history far more completely than Abela could. Not that we can disentangle them with Abela's assurance: who, for instance, can say whether those who start the Directory with the name *Abdillah* came direct from Africa or went first to Spain with the Moors and then to Malta under the reign of

Aragon? Oldest of all the names, and still abundant, are those classified by Aquilina as Early Semitic: *Borg, Caruana, Agius* (four columns), *Mifsud, Gauci*. Old Indo-European are represented by such as *Tonna* and *Vella*; the later Siculo-Italian are too numerous to cite. The Jewish contribution is varied and widespread; it begins with *Abela* (which would have appalled our noble historian) and includes such everyday Maltese surnames as *Attard, Azzopardi* (supposedly descendants of Sephardic Jews), *Bernard, Degiorgio, Micallef*. 'New' Indo-European names such as *Gollcher, Brockdorf, Strickland, de Trafford, Schranz*, are well-rooted transplants of the 19th century, as are the abundance of names derived from the Army and Royal Navy. To this grand cosmopolitan drum-roll, which ends with eight columns of *Zammit* and can stand comparison with the directories of the great cities of America, the latter-day Smiths, Joneses, and Robinsons of the United Kingdom and the Commonwealth are adding their quota. Known to Englishmen who are obliged to stay at home as 'The Tax-Dodgers' and to the Maltese as 'Sixpenny Settlers' or, more sardonically, 'White Settlers', they have yet to earn the title given them by a Maltese wit, 'This Happy Breed', and only time can tell whether at least a proportion of their surnames will be as digestible and familiar as *Abdillah* and *Zammit*.

'Where are the noble names today?'

ANGRY VISITOR: THE LANDSCAPE AND D. H. LAWRENCE

The second useful bit of information that comes to us from Abela's interest in noble families is about the places they lived in and, in consequence, the picture his descriptions provide of 17th century and medieval Malta. The Knights had been building in Renaissance and Baroque for almost a century when Abela wrote his *Discrittione*, but most of the Malta he knew was unaffected by this, and the world he described was medieval, Siculo-Norman, relatively unassuming, and of low elevation. Though born in the new capital of Valletta in 1582, when Verdala was Grand Master, the historian's passion was for the old, discarded capital, known to the Arabs as Mdina, to the Aragonese as Notabile, to the Knights as Città Vecchia. To Abela, it was always 'Our City' (*Nostra Città*), lying at the very heart of Maltese history, and we must use our imagination when we inspect it if we are to get any idea of its significance to him.

We see within the Arab walls a tiny city of great antiquity, distinct, perhaps, from all other cities in the unity of its diversity: there is hardly one building that is not at peace with its neighbours.

Yet the major buildings are baroque and majestic, while the narrow side streets and former palaces are relatively small and much more ancient. We think it a wonder that there should still be houses with Norman windows, corbels, and façades, and when Abela, with his usual accuracy, tells us what coat of arms is to be seen on a particular house front, we are astonished to walk round and find it is still there, exactly as he said. But the relics that are so impressive to us as Norman and medieval survivals are only fragments of a whole that was everyday and commonplace to him, merely 'Our City' as he had always known it. What fascinated him about it was what had survived there until his own day, what remained of a far more distant past. This was embodied in the remnants of Roman and Carthaginian antiquity, the fragments of the city as it had been more than a thousand years before his time:

'At the entrance to the main gate, the townspeople have preserved a statue made of local marble . . . it stands seven and a half palms high . . . and across the breast are two birds cut in the likeness of peacocks, creatures sacred to Juno . . . the tutelary goddess of the city . . .within the gates, in all the streets, one sees marble columns, some complete and some in fragments, and cornices, pedestals, and capitals, and other remains of ancient materials which time has not managed to devour. What they have endured is a credit to what went into the making of them, for if the locals had their way, they would be utterly destroyed, along with many other similar and more wonderful things belonging to the revered antiquity of Our City—lost, ruined, held of no account, and scarcely acknowledged.'

We are reminded here of Abela's contemporary, John Aubrey, lamenting the passing of the antiquities of England. Disrespect for ancient things was even more pervasive in their time than it is in our own. Today, we have protective societies; Abela's day had only exceptional individuals. He himself was not only the 'Father of Maltese History' but the father of Maltese antiquities, and their first curator. In the museum that was his house near Valletta, he collected and hoarded every relic that came his way—coins, statues, carvings, reliefs, sections of columns and pedestals. In addition, he had, we are told, a 'prodigious Quantity' of 'minerals, snakes, funghi, petrified dates, testaceans, sepulchral urns, lamps . . . fragments of mummies, clay Etruscan vases' and large numbers of old coins and medals. Within a hundred years of his death, his collection was 'lost, ruined, held of no account'; even the museum itself, with its gardens and grottoes, was disappearing as if it had never been. Today, all that remains of this excellent man's antiquarian labours is a fine statue of Hercules and a large relief bearing the heads of Penthisilea, Claudia, Tullia, and Zenobia. Both are in the little Roman museum outside 'Our City'. The Hercules looks little the worse for having had its head sawn off by a thief in the 18th century and peddled in the streets of Valletta. But it is of no account, anyway, because, like the large relief, it is not Classical at all. The old collector is survived only by two fakes.

The fate of Abela's collection is not unusual: all over the world, all the things one man collects with pride and devotion are devoured by time, neglect, fire, and heirs. But Malta is perhaps unique in that no other country has so much concealed underground and so little to show for it on the surface. What is not used in Malta does not fall into ruin, it just disappears. Shaped stone is the only building material, and it can always be used again. Megaliths, which are almost impossible to move and impractical to build with, may remain in situ for thousands of years, but ruins and neglected houses are incorporated very quickly into terraces, field walls and farm buildings. Pieces of ancient columns, cornices, and pedestals come to the same end, as do the smaller stones of pre-historic buildings: in Gozo, for example, every piece of an ancient stone circle has 'survived', in that each is part of a farmer's walls. The long defensive wall built a century ago by the British, 'The Victoria Line', has never been breached by an invader but is proving irresistible to farmers and builders. In Malta, the only safe ruin is the invisible one—the ruin that is covered with soil in the making of a field, or hidden under a new town. The riches that lie underground in this little island are too vast even to guess at; 'Our City' is said to be merely the seventh of its sort, and outside its walls a whole Roman town lies buried.

Church of Tal-Hlas, near Zebbuġ

Meanwhile, the country walker can observe continually the two curious processes—the slow disappearance day by day of a neglected building, as its blocks are mysteriously removed night by night; and the slow burial below ground of ancient sites. Punic tombs, for example, are popular rubbish dumps: it takes little more than a year or two to fill one to ground level with paper, carcases, household rubbish, and unwanted rubble: in this way, the grave rises out of sight as readily as the neglected house descends, and the surface of the land resumes its rough ancient appearance.

The British contribution to rural ugliness has been immense, and extremely well received; the rusty coils of barbed wire discarded by the soldier are laid proudly on top of field walls by the farmer; backed by a hedge of prickly-pear, and intermingled with broken beer bottles, they would make any Turk hesitate to ravish the inhabitants. Old oil-drums are also immensely popular; in an island that has no wood, a row of upended drums makes an excellent gate, easily rolled aside when the farmer himself wants to use the roadway: when well rusted, they can also be bashed flat and worked in with the barbed wire and broken glass on the wall tops. One exceptionally beautiful area in the south-east of the island has been devoted exclusively to the leavings of the Tin Age; rusting tins, numbering millions, serve as a broad, brown verge to some two of three miles of cart-roads. The Plastic Age, which we are now entering, has already made a sizeable contribution to the landscape, but its bloated containers, toilet accessories, and armless dolls have far to go before they overwhelm the honest tin.

Malta's debt to the infidel Corsairs has not been acknowledged by her historians. But it is thanks entirely to those marauders that this tiny island has so large an area of countryside. Terror of pirates made a townsman even of the farmer; though he worked his lands by day, he returned to a town safely inland at night. Many an old settlement that proved to be too close to the coast exists today in name only, wiped off the map when the villagers abandoned it, leaving only a small, medieval church behind them. Thus, while the inland towns grew, swallowing many hamlets as they did so, a green belt grew proportionately larger, only dotted with the

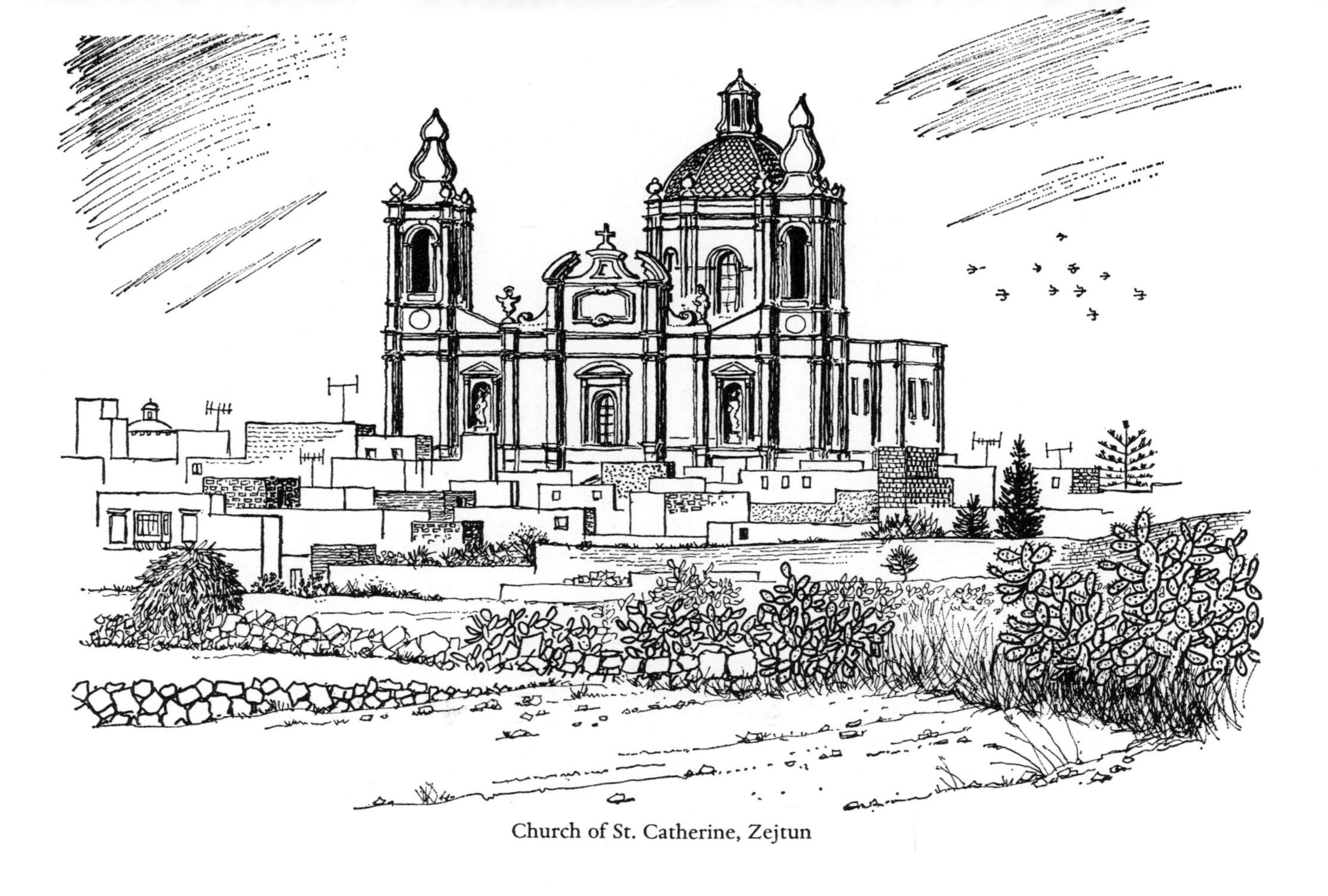

Church of St. Catherine, Zejtun

charming stone cubes that housed the farmer's tackle and some of his stock, but never the farmer himself. This situation changed once the infidel ceased to be a menace, but by then the pattern was established. It gives Malta its peculiar triple charm—that of the countryside, which constitutes nine-tenths of its area; that of the town; and that of the curious blending of the two that may be seen in Mr. Lancaster's drawing of the Church of St. Catherine in Zejtun. There, as in Mdina, the Baroque arises in splendour out of far more ancient foundations; but whereas Mdina had always the stamp of a city and grew its Baroque out of a medieval township, lesser places like Zejtun are much closer to the countryside, and the little cubes that surround their churches derive from a far more rural, far more ancient way of life. It is difficult to say how ancient this derivation is, because much of the building was done under the protection of the Knights, but in a manner that was already traditional.

This manner is appropriate, inflexible, and capable of infinite repetition. It is based on the simple fact that where there is no timber to make beams, all roofs must be of solid stone and provision made, in the walling, to support the weight above. This support is provided by very thick walls into which heavy arches are deeply imbedded, sometimes down to ground level, as in the little chapel at Maqluba. These arches, in turn, support the slabs of the ceiling. The distance between the arches, in any given length of building, is decided absolutely by the invariable nature of the slabs above; these cannot be more than seven feet long, or they may crack and split, succumbing to summer heat, occasional earth tremors, and their own weight. Two of their seven feet must rest on the flat tops of each pair of arches; thus, there can never be more than five feet of ceiling between arches, and the arches themselves must always be at least two feet in width. Out of these plain necessities, the room of the characteristic Maltese farm building, the older type of church, and the simple town house have grown—always a cube, to sustain the heavy arches; always preponderantly arched, to sustain the slabs; always flat roofed, to avoid the extra weight of a dome. So engrained is this method that even where the architect has risked a slight rising curve in his roof, the better to throw off storm-water, he has been careful to edge his roof with a low parapet that hides the curve, thus maintaining at least the appearance of the severe tradition.

The whole countryside and the verges of the country towns are flecked with these charming little cubes. Often, half a dozen are arranged together in a square, with a courtyard in the centre onto which most of the doors and windows open. Is this type wholly indigenous or was it brought from elsewhere? It gives a most particular appearance to the landscape, distinguishing it entirely from Sicily and Calabria, on the one hand, and, on the other, from the world of little domes that characterises Jerusalem and the turretted buildings of Morocco. The buildings of Tunisia are thought by some to be closest to the Maltese, but in the opinion of the principal authority on Maltese architecture,† the style derives probably from ancient Syria, where this characteristic use of slabs on arches seems to have originated. In short, it is perhaps of Phoenician extraction in Malta, and was a thousand years old when it arrived.

Phoenician building, then, in a landscape that was shaped, perhaps, by the same people. Diodorus Siculus tells us that it was the Phoenicians who taught the Maltese the art of agriculture, and the terracing of fields with stone walls. Ovid even says that the Phoenicians brought the very soil of the Maltese fields from Africa; this, up to a point, is possible, in that even in the time of the Knights, ships took Maltese stone away in ballast and returned with the equivalent in soil. But such foreign earth can only have been a small part of the whole: as the walker goes beside these ancient fields, he can find in the colour of the soil 'indubitable evidence' that it is made of the washings away and the crushings of the surrounding stone and clays, a dead-white in the case of the latter, rose and rich red in the case of the former, where the yellow stone has oxidised.

Malta is all stone, and much of the stone is soft, porous, frangible. The hard, dusty landscape with its stone cubes, often without a

† Quentin Hughes; *The Buildings of Malta* (1967).

single tree to relieve it, is what the summer traveller finds, and traced all over it, as with a wandering finger, is mile upon mile of free-stone walling, as varied in height, type, and course as the hedgerows of England. Scores of oil-painters have struggled to show this landscape 'in depth', but never with much success, however much they have resorted to pushing pats of butter on the canvas with their thumbs and smearing splodges of orange and blue with sweeps of the palette knife. The work of Edward Lear and other water-colourists suggest that the opposite method is the best: it is the light touch and the thin wash that render both the weight and colour.

The charm of this landscape is beyond description, in that it is seen at once or never seen at all. The advance party sent out by the Knights to report on Malta as an alternative to Rhodes was appalled by the barrenness of it all and could cite only the splendid harbours as a favourable point. These harbours, built up by the Knights into bastions and cities, were the first glimpse that a later and more unlikely visitor, D. H. Lawrence, had of the island when he visited it by ferry from Syracuse. Approached from the sea, as it always should be but rarely is today, the sight is one of the most astonishing in the world and almost justifies the clerical school in its insistence on Malta as the last bastion of Christianity. It rises out of the Mediterranean like some wonder from the sea in classical legend: at once lemon-yellow and pale grey, often with a pinkish glow, it makes the volcanic stone of Syracuse seem infinitely shabby and grimy by comparison. On deck in the early morning, Lawrence saw this beauty immediately: 'the sun rising up in a gorgeous golden rage, and the sea so blue, so fairy blue . . . a rocky, pale yellow island with some vineyards, rising magical out of the swift blue sea . . . rocks almost as pale as butter . . . islands . . . like golden shadows loitering in the midst of the Mediterranean . . .' Soon, there came into view 'the heaped glitter of the square facets of houses, Valletta, splendid above the Mediterranean . . .'†

† The D. H. Lawrence quotations are from his Introduction to *Memoirs of the Foreign Legion* by M. M. (Maurice Magnus), Martin Secker, 1924, by courtesy of Lawrence Pollinger Ltd. and the Estate of the Late Mrs. Frieda Lawrence and William Heinemann Ltd. in whose publication *Phoenix* the Introduction has been reprinted.

A rhapsody, in fact, and for once an accurate rhapsody. It carried Lawrence on its wave right into the middle of Valletta, where 'a military band . . . playing splendidly in the bright, hot morning' actually caused him to exclaim: 'One felt the splendour of the British Empire, let the world say what it likes'. What the world liked to say was soon said by Lawrence, who quickly found that the conjunction of his native Empire with Christianity's last outpost was too horrible to bear. It was the last week of May; the rains were long since over; all that remained outside Valletta was a 'bone-dry, hideous island,' all 'stone, and bath-brick dust. All the world might come here to sharpen its knives.' Friends took him on a tour—which was the last straw:

> 'we dodged about in the car upon that dreadful island, first to some fearful and stony bay, arid, treeless, desert, a bit of stony desert by the sea, with unhappy villas and a sordid, scrap-iron front: then away inland up long and dusty roads, across a bone-dry, bone-bare, hideous landscape. True, there was ripening corn, but this was all of a colour with the dust-yellow, bone-bare island. Malta is all a pale, softish, yellowish rock, just like bath-brick: this goes into fathomless dust. And the island is as stark as a corpse, no trees, no bushes even: a fearful landscape, cultivated, and weary with ages of weariness, and old weary houses here and there.'

Of Abela's beloved place, 'Our City', he could admit only that it was 'interesting'.

> [It] 'stands on a bluff of hill in the middle of the dreariness, looking at Valletta in the distance, and the sea. The houses are all pale yellow, and tall, and silent, as if foresaken. There is a cathedral, too, and a fortress outlook over the sun-blazed, sun-dried, disheartening island. Then we dashed off to another village and climbed a church dome that rises like a tall blister on the plain, with houses round and corn beyond and dust that has no glamour, stale, weary, like bone-dust, and thorn hedges sometimes, and some tin-like prickly pears. In the dusk we came round St. Paul's Bay, back to Valletta.'

Every word of this is accurate. Lawrence may not have understood human beings, but his sympathy for animals and his observations of landscapes make one mourn the fact that he persisted in writing about people. Malta in early summer is exactly as he describes it: all the spring harvest is in, and the green oases of marrow-plants, tomatoes, and vines only appear when summer is at its height. Lawrence's constant repetitions—'bone-dry', 'bone-bare'—are well chosen, because it is as a skeleton that Malta enters the summer months. In northern countries, the flesh comes off the bones in wintertime: the trees become black and bare, the grass old and frost-bitten; the shape and structure of the land becomes the dominant feature, and the tip of every bony twig is examined for the buds that will put flesh and blood on the skeleton again. But in Malta, this state of affairs is entirely reversed; it is winter that incarnates the landscape and spring that eventually reduces it to a skeleton.

Those who love northern winters because they believe that truth is in the bone-structure, not in the flesh, might see Malta in June with the same affectionate eye, for then, nothing is left to be classed as superficial and transitory. There are only the endless stone walls, the burnt and bare fields, the utterly dry earth and the interminable dust. Here is what we and Lawrence can 'see with our own eyes'—the skeleton's 'indubitable evidence' of its existence. But as with history, it is the observer's eye that scans the evidence and his mind that sums it up. To Lawrence in 1920, the 'indubitable evidence' of a 'fearful island' was plain to see: it was to be some years before New Mexico trained his eye to appreciate desert and stone, and even to bring out in him a marked, if morbid, respect for sharp knives. He was not long enough in Malta to adjust himself to African seasons: he expected the only Nature he knew, providing a well-frozen skeleton, not a baked one. He was much too offended by the desert to notice its beauties; like hundreds of thousands of simple soldiers and sailors before him, he only suffered in the glare of the 'gorgeous sun' and cursed the aridity. This is understandable; Malta is not Nottinghamshire. It is not even Tuscany, whose beauties Lawrence described so admirably;

moreover, whatever Abela may say to the contrary, it is closer to Africa than Sicily. Except from bathing-beauties and sun-tanners, the summer asks patience and understanding: it has, but in its own way, the long strain of a northern winter and the same expectations of resurrection. It demands very early rising, siestas in the afternoon, and long walks in the cool of the evening, when the skeleton may be examined closely and sympathetically and the whole structure of the terraced landscape seen in the extraordinary variety of changing lights. It is not an island for bad-tempered people, as is evident in the kindness and good manners of the Maltese. Nor is it for people who cannot wait: the Maltese are the only Mediterranean people who believe, like the British, that the forming of queues is the most upright of means to an end.

Spring comes to this inverted winter in October. It is as exciting as any northern spring and the transformation it brings about is just as complete. Hunger for the first rains is as natural to Africa as hunger for the first suns to the pale Swede: the most striking difference is the speed with which the rain does its work in a hot country and the slowness with which the sun gains strength in a cold one. By November, the skeleton of Malta is hardly visible, and the marvel of this spring is that it is so much longer than that of the north. The whole winter, so-called, is a long spring, persisting until April.

The ploughing and planting of the land in September and October is the first step in showing that the 'ages of weariness' are only, in fact, the long siesta of the summer. Two sorts of plough are to be seen, not so much ploughing the soil as stirring it. One is the traditional plough that is as old as the Romans, the Carthaginians, even, perhaps, the Phoenicians. It is no more than a stout pointed stick with an iron sock over the end of it. To it are attached a handle and a cross-bar: the farmer pushes down on the handle while a mule, or a donkey, or a horse, or an ox, or a wife and a daughter, or any mixed pair of these, pull forward on the cross-bar. Only the fields in the plains are squares or oblongs; the terraced fields of the numerous hillsides are shaped simply as nature and the farmer were obliged to make them—ovals, bulges, crescents, irregular rectangles, strips. In the relatively tiny spaces provided by these, and working always within stone walls that follow the outlines of the spaces, the ploughman traces out his incomparable designs. The why and wherefore of the patterns he makes is not to be understood by the layman; it is governed by intimate matters of contour, depth of soil, shape of ground, and receptivity to rain and well-water that only the farmer can work out. The observer's joy is simply to take up his stand in a high place and look at the results. What he sees is not so much farmland as allotments—hundreds of them forming a medley of patterns that turns the whole landscape into an extraordinary patchwork quilt, marked out in tiny, concentric circles, little squares, chessboards, and parallel curves. The ploughed land is one of the greatest beauties of Malta: to describe it properly one would need the genius and the passion for monotonous repetition of D. H. Lawrence.

The second sort of plough is the spluttering little rotary hoe, which seems to have been invented precisely for these tiny fields. It replaces the children who have fled to the factories and hotels and does the week's work of six daughters in half a morning. It is the greatest boon that has come to the Maltese farmer since Roman days, and even the most stubborn enemy of progress would not deny the farmer his gift. Work on those hot, stony fields is hard and exhausting; the old plough is little more than an extension of the farmer's own arm and he must use one hand to control his yoke-animals, stopping and turning them every half-minute in those minute spaces. One must be very romantically minded to find beauty in so much bestial effort and to deplore the arrival of the efficient little machine.

By Christmastime the transformation of the island is complete. Except in the built-up areas which form so small a part of the whole, the skeleton has had all the dust washed off it and has become a healthy, lively body. All the fields are green with their spring crops, and in the valleys where there are carobs, olive-groves, oranges, tangerines, and lemons, the general effect is almost lush. The bonework is still strongly apparent in the stone walls and uncultivated hillsides, but these could never be described as bone-dry or barren, as they help to produce the abundance of wild flowers that makes Malta a paradise for the walker and the botanist. From November until April there is every sort of narcissus, iris, and crocus, wild marigolds, snapdragons, herbs, pimpernels, mallows, geraniums, euphorbias, stonecrops, alyssum, anemones—to mention only a handful out of a huge treasury of flowers. In April, whole tracts of bare rock are almost covered with varieties of bee orchids and tiny nut irises; some stones seem to be virtually painted crimson with the cochineal-coloured sedum. The so-called 'English Weed'—an escapee from South Africa that has taken the whole island for its province—smothers the verges with pale yellow flowers, sharing them with blue borage.

'It was a lovely, lovely morning of hot sun. Butterflies were flapping over the rosemary hedges and over a few little red poppies, the young vines smelt sweet in flower . . . the corn was tall and green, and there was still some wild rose-red gladiolus flowers among the watery green of the wheat . . .'

So Lawrence, of Taormina in April, but all of which he could have seen just as well in the fields of that 'dreadful island' to the south.

It is history, climate and local conditions that have made the difference between the landscape of Malta and that of eastern Sicily. Much that is open to the eye in Sicily is walled up against the north-west wind in Malta. Row upon row of Maltese houses show only a blank front; the gardening is done in the sheltered courtyards inside. Sea-gales and Saracens between them have walled off multitudes of beauties and there have been no tourists, as in Taormina, to create a demand for shade-trees and decorative shrubs. To plant these now, in a fortress island that had no need of them before, is a long, slow work; but there is no doubt that it can be done. The place-names alone indicate that there was once wooded areas of pine, ilex, juniper, olive, and mulberry; Abela lists these, but only to add, as a rule, that no trace of the patronymic tree remains. One extraordinary exception is the area called Ghajn Ballut (the Spring of the Oaks); there, Abela tells us, we may find the ilex still—and so we may to this very day. That many of the houses and memorials he mentions are still to be seen is not nearly so astonishing as is the vision of Ghajn Ballut, with the spring water pouring out of the cliffside and evergreen oaks of vast size clustered below it. A few of these trees are thought by botanists to be as much as a thousand years old; saplings when the Normans came. More important is the evidence they provide of what the soil of Malta can sustain—a suggestion of what large parts of it might look like after half a century of determined re-afforestation. At present, most of such determination is going into planting hotels and villas: their sole contribution to the landscape is that of more stone, the intrusion of concrete, and a steady lowering of the water-table.

CATASTROPHES IN CONCRETE

The history of Malta is often described as the history, in small, of the whole of Europe. The ages of man from the New Stone Age onwards may be found in this one small place, accurately indicating the rise and fall of the western cultures with the exception of the Greek. Microcosmic, too, are certain other universal habits of a more amusing sort. One is the shrinkage of distance, to which even the settler adapts himself very quickly, so that parts of the island that are only seven miles away from him become 'too far', or 'such a long way', and even 'a hell of a trek'. The sister island of Gozo is only twenty minutes off by boat, but it is still felt to be a faraway land, inhabited by very odd people. Even in Malta itself, those who live in the north-east area, a strip some eight miles long containing the larger towns, have uncomfortable feelings about the inhabitants of the rural south-east. These rustics are not thought to be really Maltese; they are not considered to be 'nice' people, and the settler is warned against going to live in their neighbourhood. This prejudice is felt so strongly that one wonders sometimes if it rests on more than the division between north and south, or urban and rustic, that is common to all countries—if, perhaps, the people of the south-east did come of a different stock in some remote time. Whatever the case, those of the north-east remain settled in their belief and may never see the villages of the south-east in all their lifetime. This has helped enormously in the preservation of what is the largest rural area, and one of the most beautiful.

The sadder microcosm that Malta represents is that of the 'progress' that is ruining so much of the world. This process of destruction has a special poignancy in Malta's case.

This is a country that is enjoying independence for the first time in its known history, and being obliged to assess this new status

Birżebbuġa. One of the Knights' coastal redoubts showing the hand of progress

with a puzzled eye that easily becomes bloodshot. The unpleasant truth that must be swallowed first is that the beauties of the country were created and preserved by its foreign enemies and conquerors, not by its inhabitants. It was the Saracens, as has been said, who obliged the Maltese to congregate in inland towns, thus ensuring that seven-eighths of the land should remain unoccupied and unspoilt. It was the Knights who concentrated their attention on the coastal defences and religious edifices of the island, leaving nothing worse behind them than the majesty of Valletta, the baroque manner, and the isolated forts and watch-towers that are still such a feature of the coastal promontories. Their British successors took equally little interest in the rural landscape: on selected sites, their sappers built barracks of local stone: if these have no glory, they are at least solid, respectable, and digestible. Few foreigners thought of settling in the island when it was a military outpost, nor did the Maltese themselves break with their age-old habit of congregating in towns. In short, one might say that until now the beauties of Malta have depended on its military significance; they have been preserved by war.

This security has been invaded now by the horrors of peace. The terrible Turk and the Imperialist Governor have been supplanted by the smiling capitalist, armed with his deadly cheque book. The tourist and settler have been invited in with enthusiasm, to replace the sailor and the soldier and to defend the poor from unemployment. The resulting invasion, which bears no arms except money, has done more damage in five years than was ever done in five thousand.

The same may be said of many other 'unspoilt' countries of the world, but Malta is one of the few to which invasion has come quite unexpectedly as well as suddenly. It has raised the standard of living to a height undreamt of, and thanks to what a Maltese writer has called 'English gullibility for the decrepit farmhouse in a picturesque setting', it has raised the price of even the remotest piece of land to a point where only the relatively well-to-do Maltese can buy a house at all. It has brought many a bare-footed farmer riches he believed to belong only to a few fortunates in another world; nor is he the only financial beneficiary, for the lawyers, the notaries, the bankers and a horde of middlemen are thriving as never before. The farmer's sons and daughters are become the new hotel waiters and chambermaids, and it is a poor mechanic who cannot pass himself off as a whole garage. The 'old ways' of Malta, the traditions, the habits, have not the smallest hope of resisting the motor-car and the night-club: even the well-beloved village *festa*, with its stupendous accompaniment of fireworks, must reckon now with the financial risk incurred by waking up the sleeping tourist and the retired settler.

The search for a scapegoat is intensive, and ugly words such as 'neo-colonialism' and 'neo-imperialism' are visited on the foreign invaders. But the truth is that the simplest local farmer is as much engaged in the pursuit of money as the English speculator: the greedy invader finds an equally greedy fifth column waiting to greet him inside the bastions. As both the parties in the case, the English and the Maltese, would like to think that they are the country's benefactor, vast sums of hypocrisy, of which both nationals have unlimited reserves, are spent every day, and there are few profitable transactions that are not accompanied by sighs, groans, and regrets for past beauties.

Yet the villain is not the money but the expressions that the money takes. We like drawing a strong distinction between the Philistine and what we call 'the creative artist', so we are slow to understand that in all the arts today the Philistine *is* the man who aspires to be a 'creative artist'. The aim of this gentleman is not to serve his material, as an artist proper always wishes to do; it is to show that he is dissatisfied with what is ordinary, and gifted with an imaginative mind. This is most evident in what is called 'director's theatre'—the usual theatre of today—in which the director's only wish is to make of the raw material, the text, something that is peculiar to himself and able to provoke 'indubitable evidence' of his imaginative approach. Where the material is of poor quality, the attentions of a 'creative' mind do it no harm, and may even make it seem better than it is. But where the material is good, and particularly where it is simple and plain as well, 'creative' attention is far more destructive than dullness and shows far more clearly the selfishness and insensitivity of the true Philistine.

The landscape of Malta, with its little cubic forms and its natural stone, has exactly the simplicity that the 'creative mind' is best able to destroy. Destruction is not the aim, of course; just as the business-man can make all his profits look like benefactions, so can the 'creative' architect make all his depredations in a mood of benediction. Very rightly, he scorns the horrors of the ordinary, vulgar architect that are springing up all over Malta—the cheap, concrete 'villa' painted pink and blue, with the name written in icing-sugar, the balconies with their railings of twisted wire painted vermilion and ginger, the picture windows shaded by Venetian blinds of pastel plastic. He knows very well that in the clear light of this Mediterranean island where the stone is absorbed into the land-scape, one concrete structure of 'Riviera white' can be seen for miles and ruin the appearance of a whole hillside. His intention is to improve on such monstrous little insults and replace vulgarity with the productions of a thoughtful mind. Like all who aspire to be 'creative', his first need is to provide himself with a 'theme'—some intellectual theory that is sufficiently fundamental to justify extraordinary superstructures. Thus, an approach to creation that is essentially whimsical is given the appearance of one that is not merely high principled but almost austere.

The Maltese theme was provided some thirty years ago by two architects who declared that building in Malta must be done 'in the vernacular'. This theory was plain, sensible, and well-intentioned; it was no more than an indication to the young architect to study what was traditional and acceptable to the Maltese land-scape and develop his ideas harmoniously with what already existed. This would mean that a Maltese house would be recognisably such and would not give the spectator the impression that it was a part of the capital of Brazil or a laggard fragment of New Delhi.

Like all theories, that of the 'vernacular' took no account of what it was likely to suffer in 'creative' hands. These, being essentially the opposite of what they supposed themselves to be, found the nature of the 'vernacular' to lie in any oddity or peculiarity of old Maltese building that was unlike its equivalent anywhere else: as if one were to develop a language not from its old grammar but from its particular swear-words. To give a very simple example of this: water being Malta's most precious commodity, there was for centuries a wise edict requiring every builder of a new house to do so upon a large cistern, and to duct into this whatever rainwater fell upon his roof. Ecclesiastical buildings were exempted from this rule, and when Providence provided a nourishing rain it was expelled violently from the religious roof through long spouts shaped like rectangular aqueducts or the barrels of small cannons. This particular way of getting rid of something that had been better conserved was soon seen to be a 'vernacular' one, particularly as the spouts used for the same purpose in Sicily and Italy took the form of lions' mouths, or dragons'. So, set with the task of building a new hotel, the 'creative' architect was at pains to see that it should waste the maximum of water in the most Maltese way, and placed at intervals around his roofs large numbers of protruding aqueducts and streamlined cannons. The idea caught on very quickly, and today it is a poor villa that rates the conservation of water through a mundane drain-pipe higher than the wasting of it in the approved clerical 'vernacular'.

Basic to this approach is a marked childishness of thought; this is to be found in all attempts to build in the 'vernacular'. If the ancestral Maltese built megalithic temples, what more expressive of Malta than a megalithic hotel, entered between rows of dolmens? If the old churches were lit only by a small oval hole above the west door, why not small oval holes punched round a whole facade? If the great Maltese baroque architect, Girolamo Cassar, had a weakness for corners strapped up with rusticated quoins, why not quoins on your villa, as much rusticated as possible? Indeed, why not rusticate here, there, and everywhere, chipping every available trim from footings upwards, and using stones much as a farmer would—longways, shortways, angular, bulbous? As for the traditional Maltese arch, which of course could be rusticated too, what limits could be set for its 'vernacular' expression when it could spring out sideways from walls like a buttress, or preside heavily over a tiled patio, supporting nothing?

It is no wonder that what has been created in the name of the 'vernacular' appears to be the work of the spirit of parody. As has been said, the architecture of the Sappers was plain and solid, but it fitted into the landscape well enough. It never seems to cast ridicule upon its surroundings in the manner of a 'vernacular' dwelling, and it always seems to be present in order to do the work it was built for. The 'vernacular' hotel appears to have entirely the opposite intention, such as re-awakening in three hundred tourists a spirit of defunct religious devotion rather than plain satisfaction with their accommodation.

Between the two extremes of architects—he of the 'vernacular' and he of the plain vulgar—comes the middling man to whom building presents no challenge at all. His contribution to ugliness is that which is to be found in all the cities of Europe—the four-square, six-storey apartment house that suddenly arises in the middle of things on the cleared site of a hundred hovels. Such buildings are remarkable only in that they succeed in appearing in so many unlikely places. Whether the terrain is flat or steeply pitched, or marshy or rocky, or urban or rustic, they appear just the same, announcing nothing beyond the fact that since the population has risen, they have been obliged to rise too. They can also be reproduced in small and littered in large numbers over large areas, as in the case of the former beauty-spot of St. Paul's Bay. Here the founder of Maltese Christianity was shipwrecked,; and here, now, six immense oil tanks salute the occasion in coats of brilliant silver paint.

It is fair to say that many new buildings in Malta look nice enough until they are finished. So long as the creative mind can be kept retarded, the landscape can breathe freely; the horror begins only when what is plain and pleasing turns out to be the mere basis of beautiful afterthoughts. It is very sad to walk through a new area of buildings that appear to have been completed and find that they have only been started—that nothing reminiscent of a medieval farmhouse has as yet been added, or that the lower windows have not yet been surrounded with glazed tiles, or that the yellow stone has still to be painted white so as to make it seem as elegant as concrete. But the day comes at last when an old carriage lamp is fastened with beaten iron to the porch, and one knows that for many years to come, though the drains may never work, there will be safe access by night up the twisting path of multi-coloured crazy-paving.

* * * * *

The wonder is that in so small a place, so much remains. The amount that still lies buried and invisible is beyond imagination, but what is visibly astonishing is what can be seen from any high hill—almost three quarters of the whole island, surrounded by miles of blue sea and scarcely touched by the builder. There are countless byways of twisting cart-tracks and dozens of curious hills and valleys to be explored; many such places have lain unvisited and unseen for centuries except by the impassioned sportsman, whose decoys, nets and shotguns have had an effect upon the birds comparable to that of the Saracens upon the Maltese: they must fly to the towns if they are to fly at all. Half a dozen trees in the main square of Valletta house the entire winter wagtail population of Malta; but in the country, birds whose size and beauty warrant it are shot and stuffed; the smaller song-birds live out their lives in small cages hung beside the street doors. This curious reversal of the natural order—a silent countryside and singing towns—expresses a national neurosis in which barbarism appears as the only alternative to boredom. The Maltese villager lives from bang to bang, and this tendency is not likely to be corrected by legislation. The question of whether property speculators should continue to outnumber birds has been raised in Parliament and Left and Right have agreed eagerly that it shall be a non-Party issue: this is one of democracy's ways of saying that each party respects the right of the other to do nothing rather than become unpopular.

Houses, once built, are never pulled down until they become intolerable slums. Roads, once built, are never scrapped, only widened. But rubbish, which lines the old cart-tracks of Malta in unbelievable abundance, is of less durable material and could be removed without fear of infuriating the electorate. Similarly, sewage could be prevented from running down the streets, as it does in many places, without giving offence to supporters of the old folk-ways. As for trees, they could be planted in huge numbers, though it must be admitted that they would give cover to birds. Freshwater fountains, which ran copiously in Abela's day, could easily play again: to divert their water to numberless hotel lavatories that could flush as well with seawater is to suggest that the tourist's eyes are elsewhere than in his head. Finally, selected members of 'This Happy Breed' might be encouraged to settle simply because they come of the world's greatest nation of gardeners and might well disburse in flowers what they save in taxes.

But it is these people, and the casual visitors, who are likely to ruin the island in the end. One simple reason is that in a country that has a brilliant light but no trees, it is impossible to hide anything. A new 'Village' consisting of three hundred villas, complete with garages, shops, and other amenities, cannot possibly be tucked into a fold of the ground and be expected to look natural; still less can it be placed on some admirable site above the sea without bringing ruin to the rural foreground. Large villas, however good their design, cannot appear suddenly above the bay of an old fishing-village without destroying utterly the very charm and simplicity which attracted their owners in the first place.

Finally, there is the bane that is common to all warm places in the Western World today—the changed ways of those who come in their hordes from the North. Most of these, in the old days, were civil servants and traders who went to the South to work, and who usually received better pay to compensate for the greater discomfort. The sort of house that was in use among the natives suited these expatriates very well: they, too, appreciated the low bungalow with the long verandahs and the dark rooms within, or, as in Malta, the thick-walled stone cubes with few and small outside windows and all the doors opening onto a shaded central court. What they learnt from hot countries was an exotic but civilised lesson—how to stand up to the sun, how to value the shade, how to escape the glare, how to appreciate the charm of darkened rooms.

Today's settler turns this world inside out. His house cannot fit into the landscape because he places outside the very features that used to be inside. Far from avoiding the sun, or contenting himself with the fact that it is always there, he comes south to satisfy what is virtually a lust. The plain cube with its one small door and one or two small 'lights' is abhorrent to him: his front must be exposed to catch the maximum heat and glare; the glass doors and larger windows of the court must be dragged out and placed in the outer walls. A small balcony of local stone, large enough to harbour two local gossips in the cool of an evening, is totally inadequate for him: he must run his balcony round his whole front, making sure, however, that it does nothing to prevent the sun from penetrating as far as possible into the rooms behind. Far from regarding his roof as a place for catching rainwater, he sees it only as a place on which to spreadeagle his blanched visitors, who cannot afford to go back to the North without showing 'indubitable evidence' that they have been to the South. That this attitude to the Mediterranean is as vulgar and disgusting as overeating is simply a matter of opinion; what is a fact is that no southern landscape can satisfy it without destroying itself. For it is not only the private villas, the new model 'Villages' (a 'vernacular' term), that indulge it, but the dozens of massive hotels that dump themselves in 'scenic' places, hideously courting the sun and glare with their monstrous fronts.

Just as locusts never leave an area until they have eaten every square foot of it, so developers only move on when they have built to the point where it is unprofitable to stay, when what they began as villas have, as a result of over-production, started to lose their value and decline into slums. Thus, the departure of the developer is also a sure sign that the landscape is now fit for nothing and that the procedure will have to be repeated in a country that is still 'unspoilt'. There is still a vast amount to be ruined in Malta, and it is hard to imagine how it might be preserved. The government is not likely to restrain any procedure that provides employment and brings in foreign capital. The eye of the Church is fixed entirely on the lusts of the flesh: resolved to clothe the naked, it takes little interest in what covers the landscape. The indignation of *Din L'Art Helwa*—the vigorous, impoverished society to which this short book is dedicated—is the only real barrier, but like all protective societies it must first lose its fear of being dubbed 'obstructive' and 'reactionary' by those who are dedicated to buying cheap and selling dear. No society can try to save a country from ruin without being accused of wanting to destroy its capacity for development and progress; consequently, all such accusations should be seen as sure signs that the society is doing its work well. A spirit of co-operation is the last thing that should be extended to locusts and developers.

As it is usual to end books of this sort on what is called 'a note of hope', an effort to strike one or two such notes is in order here.

At least two bodies, *Din L'Art Helwa* and the Planning Area Permit Board of the Public Works Department, are strongly committed to conservation and have done much already to preserve the rural areas. They have arrived much too late to save places that must have been of great beauty at one time and the disfiguring of which is still proceeding as fast as the developers can push it: whole miles of coast in the area of St. Paul's Bay, for example, have been hideous for so long that it would be a waste of time to try and stop them becoming more hideous yet. It is more practical to regard them as an incurable disease and see their six-storey flats and slatternly villas in the light of insanitary patients who are acceptable provided they remain where they are and have no consort with the outside world. For the rest, though hotels are difficult to control, because they promise employment and riches in return for their disfigurement of beauty spots, private houses can be kept in check, and much is being done to prevent the countryside from looking as if it were spotted with eyesores.

At the time of writing, a considerable slump in the tourist traffic is affecting the building industry and so striking a fairly strong note of hope. Many developments of extremely unpleasant promise are lying unfinished and unbought; the fall in their monetary value can mean only a proportionate rise in their value as a warning to later speculators. It is ungenerous, of course, to hope that the slump will become worse, but economic depression seems about the only reliable note of hope in the matter of saving a countryside nowadays. It is too late now, for instance, for Malta to recall the Saracens to beat the builders: the Saracens have their own beauties to despoil and no time to spend on Malta's. Famine and plague, which worked wonders in the past, are also hard to find today, unless one travels East at great expense. The major hope, consequently, can only be of a stupendous, world-wide, economic catastrophe, which would certainly make sun-bathing seem frivolous and quickly reduce the new buildings of Malta to ruin. It may be too optimistic and even romantic to hope for so much, but it is heartening to think of what might follow—to picture handfuls of small, dark, Phoenician figures prying apart the fallen ashlars of the Bedrooms of the Sun and re-erecting them in the true vernacular.